★ WELCOME BABY ★

GUESTS

NAME AND RELATIONSHIP TO PARENTS

_____

_____

ADVICE FOR PARENTS

_____

_____

_____

WISHES FOR BABY

_____

_____

_____

GUESTS

NAME AND RELATIONSHIP TO PARENTS

_____

_____

ADVICE FOR PARENTS

_____

_____

_____

WISHES FOR BABY

_____

_____

_____

GUESTS

NAME AND RELATIONSHIP TO PARENTS

_____

_____

ADVICE FOR PARENTS

_____

_____

_____

WISHES FOR BABY

_____

_____

_____

GUESTS

NAME AND RELATIONSHIP TO PARENTS

_____

_____

ADVICE FOR PARENTS

_____

_____

_____

WISHES FOR BABY

_____

_____

_____

GUESTS

NAME AND RELATIONSHIP TO PARENTS

_____

_____

ADVICE FOR PARENTS

_____

_____

_____

WISHES FOR BABY

_____

_____

_____

GUESTS

NAME AND RELATIONSHIP TO PARENTS

_____

_____

ADVICE FOR PARENTS

_____

_____

_____

WISHES FOR BABY

_____

_____

_____

GUESTS

NAME AND RELATIONSHIP TO PARENTS

_____

_____

ADVICE FOR PARENTS

_____

_____

WISHES FOR BABY

_____

_____

_____

GUESTS

NAME AND RELATIONSHIP TO PARENTS

_____

_____

ADVICE FOR PARENTS

_____

_____

_____

WISHES FOR BABY

_____

_____

_____

GUESTS

NAME AND RELATIONSHIP TO PARENTS

_____

_____

ADVICE FOR PARENTS

_____

_____

_____

WISHES FOR BABY

_____

_____

_____

GUESTS

NAME AND RELATIONSHIP TO PARENTS

_____

_____

ADVICE FOR PARENTS

_____

_____

_____

WISHES FOR BABY

_____

_____

_____

GUESTS

NAME AND RELATIONSHIP TO PARENTS

_____

_____

ADVICE FOR PARENTS

_____

_____

WISHES FOR BABY

_____

_____

_____

GUESTS

NAME AND RELATIONSHIP TO PARENTS

_____

_____

ADVICE FOR PARENTS

_____

_____

_____

WISHES FOR BABY

_____

_____

_____

GUESTS

NAME AND RELATIONSHIP TO PARENTS

_____

_____

ADVICE FOR PARENTS

_____

_____

_____

WISHES FOR BABY

_____

_____

_____

GUESTS

NAME AND RELATIONSHIP TO PARENTS

_____

_____

ADVICE FOR PARENTS

_____

_____

WISHES FOR BABY

_____

_____

_____

GUESTS

NAME AND RELATIONSHIP TO PARENTS

_____

_____

ADVICE FOR PARENTS

_____

_____

_____

WISHES FOR BABY

_____

_____

_____

GUESTS

NAME AND RELATIONSHIP TO PARENTS

_____

_____

ADVICE FOR PARENTS

_____

_____

_____

WISHES FOR BABY

_____

_____

_____

GUESTS

NAME AND RELATIONSHIP TO PARENTS

_____

_____

ADVICE FOR PARENTS

_____

_____

_____

WISHES FOR BABY

_____

_____

_____

GUESTS

NAME AND RELATIONSHIP TO PARENTS

_____

_____

ADVICE FOR PARENTS

_____

_____

_____

WISHES FOR BABY

_____

_____

_____

GUESTS

NAME AND RELATIONSHIP TO PARENTS

_____

_____

ADVICE FOR PARENTS

_____

_____

_____

WISHES FOR BABY

_____

_____

_____

GUESTS

NAME AND RELATIONSHIP TO PARENTS

_____

_____

ADVICE FOR PARENTS

_____

_____

_____

WISHES FOR BABY

_____

_____

_____

GUESTS

NAME AND RELATIONSHIP TO PARENTS

_____

_____

ADVICE FOR PARENTS

_____

_____

WISHES FOR BABY

_____

_____

GUESTS

NAME AND RELATIONSHIP TO PARENTS

_____

_____

ADVICE FOR PARENTS

_____

_____

_____

WISHES FOR BABY

_____

_____

_____

GUESTS

NAME AND RELATIONSHIP TO PARENTS

_____

_____

ADVICE FOR PARENTS

_____

_____

_____

WISHES FOR BABY

_____

_____

_____

GUESTS

NAME AND RELATIONSHIP TO PARENTS

_____

_____

ADVICE FOR PARENTS

_____

_____

_____

WISHES FOR BABY

_____

_____

_____

GUESTS

NAME AND RELATIONSHIP TO PARENTS

_____

_____

ADVICE FOR PARENTS

_____

_____

_____

WISHES FOR BABY

_____

_____

_____

GUESTS

NAME AND RELATIONSHIP TO PARENTS

_____

_____

ADVICE FOR PARENTS

_____

_____

_____

WISHES FOR BABY

_____

_____

_____

GUESTS

NAME AND RELATIONSHIP TO PARENTS

_____

_____

ADVICE FOR PARENTS

_____

_____

WISHES FOR BABY

_____

_____

GUESTS

NAME AND RELATIONSHIP TO PARENTS

_____

_____

ADVICE FOR PARENTS

_____

_____

_____

WISHES FOR BABY

_____

_____

_____

GUESTS

NAME AND RELATIONSHIP TO PARENTS

_____

_____

ADVICE FOR PARENTS

_____

_____

WISHES FOR BABY

_____

_____

_____

GUESTS

NAME AND RELATIONSHIP TO PARENTS

_____

_____

ADVICE FOR PARENTS

_____

_____

_____

WISHES FOR BABY

_____

_____

_____

GUESTS

NAME AND RELATIONSHIP TO PARENTS

_____

_____

ADVICE FOR PARENTS

_____

_____

_____

WISHES FOR BABY

_____

_____

_____

GUESTS

NAME AND RELATIONSHIP TO PARENTS

_____

_____

ADVICE FOR PARENTS

_____

_____

_____

WISHES FOR BABY

_____

_____

_____

GUESTS

NAME AND RELATIONSHIP TO PARENTS

_____

_____

ADVICE FOR PARENTS

_____

_____

_____

WISHES FOR BABY

_____

_____

_____

GUESTS

NAME AND RELATIONSHIP TO PARENTS

_____

_____

ADVICE FOR PARENTS

_____

_____

_____

WISHES FOR BABY

_____

_____

_____

GUESTS

NAME AND RELATIONSHIP TO PARENTS

_____

_____

ADVICE FOR PARENTS

_____

_____

_____

WISHES FOR BABY

_____

_____

_____

GUESTS

NAME AND RELATIONSHIP TO PARENTS

_____

_____

ADVICE FOR PARENTS

_____

_____

_____

WISHES FOR BABY

_____

_____

_____

GUESTS

NAME AND RELATIONSHIP TO PARENTS

_____

_____

ADVICE FOR PARENTS

_____

_____

_____

WISHES FOR BABY

_____

_____

_____

GUESTS

NAME AND RELATIONSHIP TO PARENTS

_____

_____

ADVICE FOR PARENTS

_____

_____

_____

WISHES FOR BABY

_____

_____

_____

GUESTS

NAME AND RELATIONSHIP TO PARENTS

_____

_____

ADVICE FOR PARENTS

_____

_____

WISHES FOR BABY

_____

_____

_____

GUESTS

NAME AND RELATIONSHIP TO PARENTS

_____

_____

ADVICE FOR PARENTS

_____

_____

_____

WISHES FOR BABY

_____

_____

_____

GUESTS

NAME AND RELATIONSHIP TO PARENTS

_____

_____

ADVICE FOR PARENTS

_____

_____

_____

WISHES FOR BABY

_____

_____

_____

GUESTS

NAME AND RELATIONSHIP TO PARENTS

_____

_____

ADVICE FOR PARENTS

_____

_____

_____

WISHES FOR BABY

_____

_____

_____

GUESTS

NAME AND RELATIONSHIP TO PARENTS

_____

_____

ADVICE FOR PARENTS

_____

_____

_____

WISHES FOR BABY

_____

_____

_____

GUESTS

NAME AND RELATIONSHIP TO PARENTS

_____

_____

ADVICE FOR PARENTS

_____

_____

_____

WISHES FOR BABY

_____

_____

_____

GUESTS

NAME AND RELATIONSHIP TO PARENTS

_____

_____

ADVICE FOR PARENTS

_____

_____

_____

WISHES FOR BABY

_____

_____

_____

GUESTS

NAME AND RELATIONSHIP TO PARENTS

_____

_____

ADVICE FOR PARENTS

_____

_____

_____

WISHES FOR BABY

_____

_____

_____

GUESTS

NAME AND RELATIONSHIP TO PARENTS

_____

_____

ADVICE FOR PARENTS

_____

_____

_____

WISHES FOR BABY

_____

_____

_____

GUESTS

NAME AND RELATIONSHIP TO PARENTS

_____

_____

ADVICE FOR PARENTS

_____

_____

_____

WISHES FOR BABY

_____

_____

_____

GUESTS

NAME AND RELATIONSHIP TO PARENTS

_____

_____

ADVICE FOR PARENTS

_____

_____

_____

WISHES FOR BABY

_____

_____

_____

GUESTS

NAME AND RELATIONSHIP TO PARENTS

_____

_____

ADVICE FOR PARENTS

_____

_____

WISHES FOR BABY

_____

_____

_____

GUESTS

NAME AND RELATIONSHIP TO PARENTS

_____

_____

ADVICE FOR PARENTS

_____

_____

WISHES FOR BABY

_____

_____

_____

GUESTS

NAME AND RELATIONSHIP TO PARENTS

_____

_____

ADVICE FOR PARENTS

_____

_____

_____

WISHES FOR BABY

_____

_____

_____

GUESTS

NAME AND RELATIONSHIP TO PARENTS

_____

_____

ADVICE FOR PARENTS

_____

_____

_____

WISHES FOR BABY

_____

_____

_____

GUESTS

NAME AND RELATIONSHIP TO PARENTS

_____

_____

ADVICE FOR PARENTS

_____

_____

WISHES FOR BABY

_____

_____

_____

GUESTS

NAME AND RELATIONSHIP TO PARENTS

_____

_____

ADVICE FOR PARENTS

_____

_____

_____

WISHES FOR BABY

_____

_____

_____

GUESTS

NAME AND RELATIONSHIP TO PARENTS

_____

_____

ADVICE FOR PARENTS

_____

_____

_____

WISHES FOR BABY

_____

_____

_____

GUESTS

NAME AND RELATIONSHIP TO PARENTS

_____

_____

ADVICE FOR PARENTS

_____

_____

_____

WISHES FOR BABY

_____

_____

_____

GUESTS

NAME AND RELATIONSHIP TO PARENTS

_____

_____

ADVICE FOR PARENTS

_____

_____

WISHES FOR BABY

_____

_____

_____

GUESTS

NAME AND RELATIONSHIP TO PARENTS

_____

_____

ADVICE FOR PARENTS

_____

_____

_____

WISHES FOR BABY

_____

_____

_____

GUESTS

NAME AND RELATIONSHIP TO PARENTS

_____

_____

ADVICE FOR PARENTS

_____

_____

_____

WISHES FOR BABY

_____

_____

_____

GUESTS

NAME AND RELATIONSHIP TO PARENTS

_____

_____

ADVICE FOR PARENTS

_____

_____

WISHES FOR BABY

_____

_____

_____

GUESTS

NAME AND RELATIONSHIP TO PARENTS

_____

_____

ADVICE FOR PARENTS

_____

_____

_____

WISHES FOR BABY

_____

_____

_____

GUESTS

NAME AND RELATIONSHIP TO PARENTS

_____

_____

ADVICE FOR PARENTS

_____

_____

WISHES FOR BABY

_____

_____

_____

GUESTS

NAME AND RELATIONSHIP TO PARENTS

_____

_____

ADVICE FOR PARENTS

_____

_____

_____

WISHES FOR BABY

_____

_____

_____

GUESTS

NAME AND RELATIONSHIP TO PARENTS

_____

_____

ADVICE FOR PARENTS

_____

_____

_____

WISHES FOR BABY

_____

_____

_____

GUESTS

NAME AND RELATIONSHIP TO PARENTS

_____

_____

ADVICE FOR PARENTS

_____

_____

WISHES FOR BABY

_____

_____

_____

GUESTS

NAME AND RELATIONSHIP TO PARENTS

_____

_____

ADVICE FOR PARENTS

_____

_____

_____

WISHES FOR BABY

_____

_____

_____

GUESTS

NAME AND RELATIONSHIP TO PARENTS

_____

_____

ADVICE FOR PARENTS

_____

_____

_____

WISHES FOR BABY

_____

_____

_____

GUESTS

NAME AND RELATIONSHIP TO PARENTS

_____

_____

ADVICE FOR PARENTS

_____

_____

WISHES FOR BABY

_____

_____

GUESTS

NAME AND RELATIONSHIP TO PARENTS

_____

_____

ADVICE FOR PARENTS

_____

_____

_____

WISHES FOR BABY

_____

_____

_____

GUESTS

NAME AND RELATIONSHIP TO PARENTS

_____

_____

ADVICE FOR PARENTS

_____

_____

WISHES FOR BABY

_____

_____

GUESTS

NAME AND RELATIONSHIP TO PARENTS

_____

_____

ADVICE FOR PARENTS

_____

_____

_____

WISHES FOR BABY

_____

_____

_____

GUESTS

NAME AND RELATIONSHIP TO PARENTS

_____

_____

ADVICE FOR PARENTS

_____

_____

_____

WISHES FOR BABY

_____

_____

_____

GUESTS

NAME AND RELATIONSHIP TO PARENTS

_____

_____

ADVICE FOR PARENTS

_____

_____

_____

WISHES FOR BABY

_____

_____

_____

GUESTS

NAME AND RELATIONSHIP TO PARENTS

_____

_____

ADVICE FOR PARENTS

_____

_____

WISHES FOR BABY

_____

_____

_____

GUESTS

NAME AND RELATIONSHIP TO PARENTS

_____

_____

ADVICE FOR PARENTS

_____

_____

_____

WISHES FOR BABY

_____

_____

_____

GUESTS

NAME AND RELATIONSHIP TO PARENTS

_____

_____

ADVICE FOR PARENTS

_____

_____

_____

WISHES FOR BABY

_____

_____

_____

GUESTS

NAME AND RELATIONSHIP TO PARENTS

_____

_____

ADVICE FOR PARENTS

_____

_____

_____

WISHES FOR BABY

_____

_____

_____

GUESTS

NAME AND RELATIONSHIP TO PARENTS

_____

_____

ADVICE FOR PARENTS

_____

_____

_____

WISHES FOR BABY

_____

_____

_____

GUESTS

NAME AND RELATIONSHIP TO PARENTS

_____

_____

ADVICE FOR PARENTS

_____

_____

_____

WISHES FOR BABY

_____

_____

_____

GUESTS

NAME AND RELATIONSHIP TO PARENTS

_____

_____

ADVICE FOR PARENTS

_____

_____

WISHES FOR BABY

_____

_____

_____

GUESTS

NAME AND RELATIONSHIP TO PARENTS

_____

_____

ADVICE FOR PARENTS

_____

_____

WISHES FOR BABY

_____

_____

_____

GUESTS

NAME AND RELATIONSHIP TO PARENTS

_____

_____

ADVICE FOR PARENTS

_____

_____

_____

WISHES FOR BABY

_____

_____

_____

GUESTS

NAME AND RELATIONSHIP TO PARENTS

_____

_____

ADVICE FOR PARENTS

_____

_____

_____

WISHES FOR BABY

_____

_____

_____

GUESTS

NAME AND RELATIONSHIP TO PARENTS

_____

_____

ADVICE FOR PARENTS

_____

_____

_____

WISHES FOR BABY

_____

_____

_____

GUESTS

NAME AND RELATIONSHIP TO PARENTS

_____

_____

ADVICE FOR PARENTS

_____

_____

_____

WISHES FOR BABY

_____

_____

_____

GUESTS

NAME AND RELATIONSHIP TO PARENTS

_____

_____

ADVICE FOR PARENTS

_____

_____

_____

WISHES FOR BABY

_____

_____

_____

GUESTS

NAME AND RELATIONSHIP TO PARENTS

_____

_____

ADVICE FOR PARENTS

_____

_____

WISHES FOR BABY

_____

_____

_____

GUESTS

NAME AND RELATIONSHIP TO PARENTS

_____

_____

ADVICE FOR PARENTS

_____

_____

_____

WISHES FOR BABY

_____

_____

_____

GUESTS

NAME AND RELATIONSHIP TO PARENTS

_____

_____

ADVICE FOR PARENTS

_____

_____

_____

WISHES FOR BABY

_____

_____

_____

GUESTS

NAME AND RELATIONSHIP TO PARENTS

_____

_____

ADVICE FOR PARENTS

_____

_____

WISHES FOR BABY

_____

_____

_____

GUESTS

NAME AND RELATIONSHIP TO PARENTS

_____

_____

ADVICE FOR PARENTS

_____

_____

_____

WISHES FOR BABY

_____

_____

_____

Attach Keepsakes and Pictures

★ GIFT LOG ★

GIFT LOG

GIFT RECEIVED	GIVEN BY

★ GIFT LOG ★

GIFT RECEIVED	GIVEN BY

★ GIFT LOG ★

GIFT RECEIVED	GIVEN BY

★ GIFT LOG ★

GIFT RECEIVED	GIVEN BY

★ GIFT LOG ★

GIFT RECEIVED	GIVEN BY
_____	_____
_____	_____
_____	_____
_____	_____
_____	_____
_____	_____
_____	_____
_____	_____
_____	_____
_____	_____

* GIFT LOG *

GIFT RECEIVED	GIVEN BY
_____	_____
_____	_____
_____	_____
_____	_____
_____	_____
_____	_____
_____	_____
_____	_____
_____	_____
_____	_____
_____	_____

★ GIFT LOG ★

GIFT RECEIVED	GIVEN BY

★ GIFT LOG ★

GIFT RECEIVED	GIVEN BY
_____	_____
_____	_____
_____	_____
_____	_____
_____	_____
_____	_____
_____	_____
_____	_____
_____	_____
_____	_____

GIFT RECEIVED   GIVEN BY

GIFT LOG

GIFT RECEIVED   GIVEN BY

_____   _____

_____   _____

_____   _____

_____   _____

_____   _____

_____   _____

_____   _____

_____   _____

_____   _____

_____   _____

Made in the USA
Coppell, TX
28 February 2023

13510002R00063